Riches of the Earth

Diamonds

Irene Franck and David Brownstone

GROLIER

f Scholastic Library Publishing
Danbury, Connecticut

Credits and Acknowledgments

abbreviations: t (top), b (bottom), l (left), r (right), c (center)

Image credits: Art Resource: 3 (Scala), 11 (Aldo Tutino), 12 (Victoria and Albert Museum), 13 (Pierpont Morgan Library, M.788.f.83r); CORBIS: 1b (D. Boone), 8 (Todd Gipstein), 9 (Stock Market/George B. Diebold), 21 (Japack Photo Library), 27 (L. Clarke/Craig Aurness), 29t (Lowell Georgia), 29b (Jonathan Blair); Gemological Institute of America (GIA), Inc.: 10l, 10r, 17 (Nicholas DelRe), 24; Getty Images: 4-5 (Stone/Steve Taylor), 22 (Image Bank/Marks Productions); Russell J. Hemley, Carnegie Institution: 28; National Aeronautics and Space Administration (NASA): 1t and running heads; National Geographic Society: 23 (Volkmar Wentzel); Photo Researchers, Inc.: 6 (Ken Eward/Biografx), 25 (M. Courtney-Clarke); Woodfin Camp & Associates: 19 and 20 (Jason Laure). Authors' Archives: 15, 18, 26l, 26r. Original images created for this book by K & P Publishing Services: 7t, 7b, 16, 27l.

Our thanks to Joe Hollander, Phil Friedman, and Laurie McCurley at Scholastic Library Publishing; to photo researchers Susan Hormuth, Robin Sand, and Robert Melcak; to copy editor Michael Burke; and to the librarians throughout the northeastern library network, in particular to the staff of the Chappaqua Library—director Mark Hasskarl; the expert reference staff, including Martha Alcott, Michele J. Capozzella, Maryanne Eaton, Catherine Paulsen, Jane Peyraud, Paula Peyraud, and Carolyn Reznick; and the circulation staff, headed by Barbara Le Sauvage—for fulfilling our wide-ranging research needs.

Published 2003 by Grolier
Division of Scholastic Library Publishing
Old Sherman Turnpike
Danbury, Connecticut 06816

For information address the publisher:
Scholastic Library Publishing, Grolier Division
Old Sherman Turnpike, Danbury, Connecticut 06816

Library of Congress Cataloging-in-Publication Data

Franck, Irene M.
    Diamonds / Irene Franck and David Brownstone.
      p. cm. -- (Riches of the earth ; v. 3)
    Summary: Provides information about diamonds and their many uses both in industry and as adornments.
    Includes bibliographical references and index.
    ISBN 0-7172-5730-4 (set : alk. paper) -- ISBN 0-7172-5715-0 (vol. 3 : alk paper)
      1. Diamonds--Juvenile literature [1. Diamonds.] I. Brownstone, David M. II. Title.

TN990.F73 2003
622'.382--dc21

2003044079

Printed in the United States of America

Designed by K & P Publishing Services

Contents

Fire and Ice

Fire and ice—that's what many people call diamonds. "Fire" refers to the brilliant colors and light that sparkle and flash in the cut gems. "Ice" refers to a diamond's hardness and clearness (like everyday ice) and also to its coolness against the skin (because it absorbs heat). Whatever they are called, diamonds are some of the most beautiful and valuable materials in the world.

Diamonds are so highly prized because they have some very special qualities. Diamond is the hardest material known. Nothing can scratch a diamond except another diamond. A diamond (positioned properly) can even pierce a sheet of steel. No acid or other harmful substance is strong enough to damage a diamond.

That doesn't mean diamonds

Diamond or Diamonds?

A single stone is called a diamond. Several stones are called diamonds. However, the material itself is called simply diamond. (In the same way, a glass you drink from is made of the material glass.)

Diamonds pack a lot of brilliance into a very little package. This small diamond (center) is being held by a pair of tweezers.

cannot be destroyed or damaged. Being made of carbon (the same substance as in charcoal on a barbecue or graphite in a pencil), diamond can burn at high temperatures. When it catches fire, the diamond's carbon quickly combines with oxygen in the air to form carbon dioxide. This colorless, odorless gas then simply floats away!

Diamonds can also be cut—and that leads to another reason they are so valued. Expertly cut diamonds do very special things with light, making diamonds sparkle like stars in the sky (see p. 9). Jewelers have developed ways of cutting diamonds to increase their brilliance (see p. 25).

Even tiny fragments of diamonds are valuable. In early times many people believed that diamonds could not be broken. Dishonest diamond buyers would sometimes smash pebbles that people brought to sell. When the pebbles broke, the sellers believed that their stones were worthless and would go away disappointed. The diamond merchants would then pocket the still-valuable fragments.

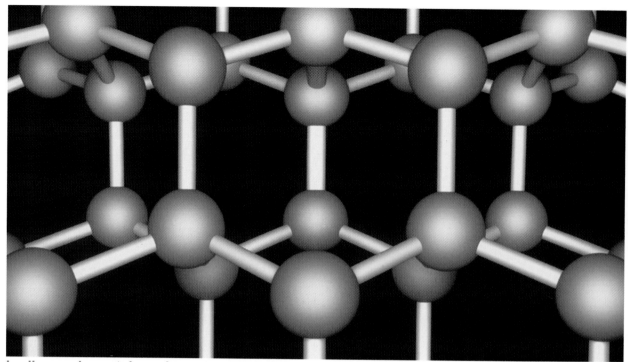

In diamond crystals carbon atoms are linked with one another—each with four others—in all directions to form a strong network. That makes diamond hard and strong.

What Are Diamonds?

Diamonds are made of carbon, one of the most common materials on Earth. Every living and nonliving thing on Earth is made from basic materials called *elements* (112 of them so far, though more are being discovered). Most things are made of combinations of elements, but pure diamond is made of just one element: *carbon* (C, for short). This means that all of a diamond's basic units—the *atoms* that are the "building blocks" of nature—are made of carbon.

Graphite (used in pencils) and diamonds are both made of pure carbon. Both are also patterned solids called *crystals*. These crystals have atoms connected to each other in regular, repeating patterns. What makes bright, clear diamond and dark, smooth graphite so different? The way they are made and the way the carbon atoms fit together.

In graphite crystals the carbon atoms form themselves into sheets, which slide against each other. This makes the graphite soft, smooth, and slippery. That's why we can write easily with a pencil.

Diamond crystals are built differently. The intense heat and pressure deep in the Earth where they are formed (see p. 17) push the carbon atoms into special formations. In diamond every carbon atom is connected with four other carbon atoms in all directions (see image on p. 6), forming a solid network.

The result is that diamond is extremely strong and hard. Many modern scientists have tried to make a harder material, but so far no one has succeeded.

Diamond Shapes

In nature diamond crystals tend to occur in some standard shapes, with flat sides. The most common shape is the *octahedron* (see below). In early times octahedron diamonds were believed to have special magi-

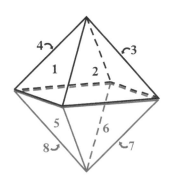

The classic diamond shape is an *octahedron*. It looks like two pyramids placed bottom to bottom. Each pyramid has four triangle (three-sided) faces on top and a square on the bottom. An octahedron diamond being cut for jewelry is often split (*cleaved*) where the "bottoms" meet. The outline of the octahedron is what we commonly call a "diamond" shape (as in a baseball diamond or the diamond symbol on a playing card).

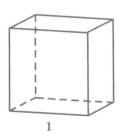
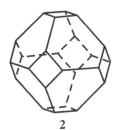
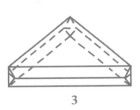
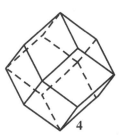

These are some other common diamond shapes:
1. *Cube*, a boxlike shape with six roughly equal sides;
2. *Cubo-octahedron*, a combination of the cube and octahedron, with sides of different sizes and shapes;
3. *Macle twin*, which is like two thick triangles (three-sided figures) placed on top of each other, additionally thickened where they meet;
4. *Dodecahedron*, a figure that has 12 roughly equal sides.

cal powers. Some other common shapes are also shown on page 7.

In the rough—that is, when found in nature—many diamonds are not so defined and regular (see image on p. 17). Some have round- ed corners from being rubbed up against each other in streambeds for long periods of time. Others were pushed out of shape while still deep in the Earth or have been broken or otherwise damaged.

What Is a Carat?

A *carat* is a measure used in weighing diamonds and other precious stones. It was created because even tiny gemstones are valuable, so measurements must be very precise.

Originally the carat was based on the weight of certain seeds, but this weight could vary from place to place. In the early 1900s most countries adopted a standard weight for the carat.

One carat equals .2 grams (200 milligrams or .007 ounces). That is only about as much as two straight pins (not safety pins)!

Even so, a carat is relatively large for an everyday diamond. The diamonds in most engagement rings weigh less than one carat. A good-quality diamond of one-half (.5) carat might sell for $2,000 or more. A diamond of a full carat might sell for three or more times as much. Prices rise even more sharply for larger diamonds because they are more rare.

An even more precise measure is the *point*. Each point equals one hundredth (.01) of a carat. (Gold and other precious metals are measured in *karats*, sometimes also spelled *carats*, but there the term refers to purity, not weight.)

Red diamonds are very rare at any size. This one, enlarged in the picture, weighs nine carats and is worth more than $2.5 million.

Color in Diamonds

The many small, flat, polished cuts (*facets*) in this diamond make it more brilliant by reflecting light and color in many directions. The rainbow of colors on the black background results from light being broken apart as it passes through the diamond.

A pure diamond in its natural state is clear and colorless. However, an expertly cut diamond flashes brilliantly, with all the colors of the rainbow.

The light we see as "white" actually includes all colors—red, orange, yellow, green, blue, violet, and every shade in between. As light passes through a clear object, colors bend at different angles. Then, at just the right angles, we see the whole range of colors. That happens in cut diamonds just as it does in a rainbow (where light passes through water droplets in the air). Also, some light meets the far side of a clear object and then is bounced (reflected) back to us, as in a window if light strikes at the right angle.

Expert diamond-cutters use these facts about light to guide them in cutting diamonds (see p. 25). They aim to cut a diamond so the finished gem shows as many colors

Once brown diamonds were mostly used in industry. However, they are now fashionable, in shades ranging from light ones called "champagne" to darker "cognac" (near left).

Color in diamonds sometimes results from small amounts of other materials mixed in with the carbon. Yellow diamonds like this one (above left) result when traces of the element nitrogen are included.

and as much light as possible. Diamonds reflect back more light than any other gemstone. This gives them "fire" and brilliance.

Fancies

Pure diamond is pure carbon. However, many diamonds have flaws, including small amounts of other substances mixed in with the carbon. These can produce colored diamonds, called *fancy diamonds* or simply *fancies*.

Brown is the most common color in diamonds. Traditionally most were unwanted for jewelry and so were used in industry. However, in the 1980s Australians—whose mines produced many brown diamonds—began a successful campaign to make them glamorous and fashionable.

Yellow is the second most common color in diamonds. Many have been found in South Africa. The largest modern cut diamond—the Golden Jubilee, weighing 545.67 carats—is colored a golden yellow.

Diamonds in the pink-red-purple color range have long been prized for their bright colors. Most early pink diamonds came from India, but the main modern source is Australia. Red and purple diamonds are much rarer.

The most desired fancies have always been blue diamonds. One called the French Blue weighed 112 carats. It was sold to France's King Louis XIV in 1669 by diamond merchant Jean-Baptiste Tavernier. Stolen in 1792, during the French Revolution, it was never seen again.

However, many diamond experts believe that the 44.5-carat Hope diamond was cut from the French Blue. Appearing from "nowhere" in 1830, the Hope was later put into a necklace and is now in the Smithsonian Institution.

The French Blue came from India, but many other notable blue diamonds have come from South Africa. Among these was the Cullinan diamond, the largest known rough diamond ever found (see p. 26).

Diamonds also occur in other colors. These include pale green, orange, gray, violet, milky white, and even black.

Some diamonds also change color. This can happen, for example, if diamonds are heated or exposed to special rays. (They can't be heated too much, however, or they will burn!)

Some rare diamonds are of one color but also show another color. Other diamonds even glow in the dark. Scientists are still exploring why such unusual things happen to color in diamonds.

One of the most famous blue diamonds is the Hope diamond, now in the Smithsonian Institution. It is shown here in its modern setting, in a necklace with 62 matched colorless diamonds.

In early times diamonds were simply polished (not cut), so their size was not reduced. This portrait by Abu'l Hassan (Nadir al-Zaman), painted in 1616 or 1617, shows India's Prince Khurran (later Moghul emperor Shah Jahan) holding a large diamond used to decorate his turban.

Diamonds in History

In early times people did not realize how beautiful diamonds could be. That is because—when found in nature—diamonds usually look like dull pebbles. Instead, people focused on other qualities of diamonds, especially their hardness.

All known early diamonds came from India. When diamonds were discovered there is unknown, but they were traded to many parts of Asia and Europe by 400 B.C. The modern name *diamond* comes from the Greek word *adamas*. (Today the word *adamant* means extremely hard.) However, Greece itself had no diamonds of its own, only those brought from India.

This image from an 1800s Turkish manuscript illustrates the legend of the Valley of the Diamonds. According to this fictional account, diamonds were guarded by snakes. To get the diamonds, people threw pieces of meat into the valley. Diamonds stuck to the meat (they are attracted by grease). When scavenging birds carried the meat out of the valley, hunters could follow them and get the diamonds.

Stories and Myths

Many stories and myths were spread about diamonds. People believed that diamonds could protect them from danger, evil, and even death. Rulers might carry diamonds as part of a sword or scepter (a stick or rod showing royal authority). Other rich and powerful people might wear diamonds on a turban or other clothing. Only later did diamonds become primarily worn as ornamental jewelry.

In a related belief diamonds were thought to cure poisoning and sickness. Sick people would sometimes be given diamonds to hold in their hands or warm in their mouths. A wealthy few were even given spoonfuls of diamond fragments to eat, and some died as a result, because hard diamonds caused internal injuries.

A different belief held that diamonds were poisonous. Some believed that pure diamonds offered cures, while those that were imperfect could kill.

Whatever their specific beliefs, all felt that diamonds were extremely valuable. This meant that a fortune awaited anyone who found a diamond.

The people who worked the Indian diamond fields apparently told stories to keep outsiders from trying to look for the precious stones. When Greek conqueror Alexander the Great was in northwestern India in 327–325 B.C., for example, he heard that the precious stones were found in a Valley of the Diamonds. There they were supposedly guarded by snakes (see p. 13).

The truth was much more ordinary. Most early diamonds were found on the banks of Indian rivers (see p. 18).

The Middle Ages

The early Romans wore some diamonds from India, bought from Persian and Arab traders. However, the diamond trade fell off as the Roman Empire declined from about 300 A.D. on.

In any case, the largest and finest diamonds were kept in India and the nearby Middle East. India remained the main source of diamonds until the 1700s, though some diamond fields were discovered in Borneo by 500 A.D.

European writers began mentioning diamonds again in the 1000s. As trade with the Middle East increased, diamonds began to reach Europe once more.

In the 1200s France's King Louis IX banned the wearing of diamonds by anyone but the king. Even so, diamonds did not begin to be featured in European royal crowns until the 1300s. Not until the 1400s would French women defy the diamond ban and begin to wear the precious stones. In these centuries cuts were developed to enhance the beauty of diamonds (see p. 25).

New Discoveries

Europe's appetite for diamonds grew enormously after the late 1490s. That was when the Portuguese opened a direct sea route around Africa. For the first time Europeans had direct access to diamonds, and large, fine stones began to make their way into Europe. However, by then India's fields were close to being mined out.

In the early 1700s new diamond fields were discovered in Brazil. This country was the main source of diamonds from about 1730 to 1870, often mined by slaves brought from Africa.

Brazilian mines produced so many diamonds that prices fell sharply in the late 1730s. For the first time diamonds began to be affordable by people outside royal and enormously wealthy families.

Slaves brought across the ocean from Africa were the main workers in the diamond mines of Brazil, watched by overseers, as in this image from a book published in the early 1800s.

South African Diamonds

The diamond world changed when major new fields were discovered in South Africa, beginning in late 1866. A diamond rush resulted. By 1872 nearly 95 percent of the world's diamonds were coming from the Kimberley and nearby mines in South Africa.

The early South African mines were divided up into hundreds of holdings, many of them tiny. Some key figures began to buy up the small holdings and then whole mines. By 1888 the main diamond mines were consolidated (put together) in a single company, the De Beers Consolidated Mining Company, still a major power in the diamond world.

The South African mines produced enormous numbers of diamonds. Wealthy people drenched and draped themselves in diamonds, and small diamonds began to be affordable by people of the middle classes. Even people who were far from wealthy began to buy diamonds, as it became fashionable for a man to buy a diamond engagement ring for the woman he intended to marry.

New Sources

Major new mines opened in Russia's Siberia in the 1950s and in western Australia in the 1970s. By the mid-1990s almost 38 percent of the world's diamond production came from Australia and more than 11 percent from Russia.

South Africa's share of the world's production was down to only about 8 percent. However, De Beers and other South African companies were active in many other diamond fields in Africa. The largest of these were in Congo (then Zaire) and Botswana, with smaller fields in Angola, Namibia, Ghana, the Central African Republic, Guinea, Sierra Leone, and Zimbabwe. The African fields altogether still accounted for nearly half of the world's diamond production.

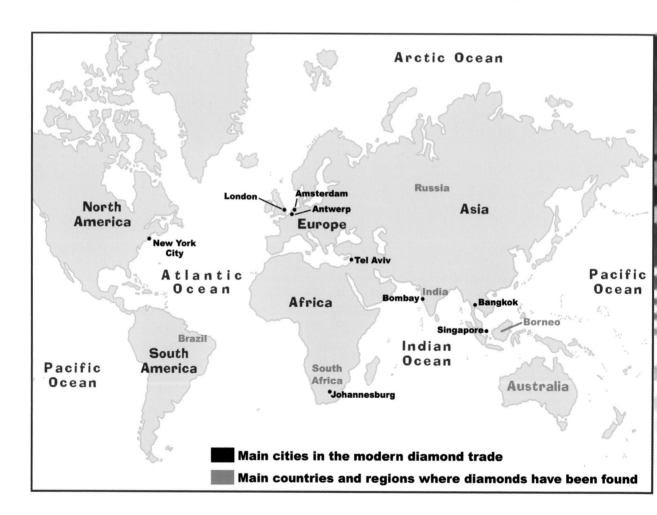

Main cities in the modern diamond trade

Main countries and regions where diamonds have been found

Diamonds "in the rough"—as they are found in nature before being polished and cut—show little of the fire and brilliance they will have when refined into gemstones.

Where Diamonds Come From

Superman once made a diamond by squeezing a lump of coal in his fist, but that was fiction. In reality it takes much more than that to form a diamond.

Most diamonds were formed deep inside the Earth. Below the crust of the Earth—the outer part we live on—lies an area called the *mantle*. That is where diamonds were created, more than 150 kilometers (93 miles) below the Earth's surface.

The mantle is very hot, more than 900 degrees Celsius (1,600 Fahrenheit). It is also under enor-

Where diamonds are found near water, miners sometimes build new pathways for some or all of the water, to expose more of the streambed for mining, as in this view from Brazil in the early 1800s.

mous pressure. The gases that surround Earth (the *atmosphere*), the crust of Earth, and everything on it all press down on the mantle. The great heat and pressure acted together to create diamonds.

The Earth's crust varies in thickness and also contains cracks and flaws. Material from the mantle sometimes pushes up into cracks in the crust, even exploding to the surface in what we call *volcanoes*. As it cools, material from the mantle forms rocks of many different types. A rock called *mica peridotite* is the main source of diamonds.

Diamond-bearing rocks often occur in long, thin tubelike formations called *kimberlite pipes*. (The name comes from South Africa's diamond-rich Kimberley fields; see p. 15.)

The crust of the Earth sometimes buckles and shifts (as in earthquakes). That can bring diamond-bearing rock near the surface. Miners dig diamonds out of these underground pipes.

However, diamonds can sometimes be found right on the Earth's surface, as in early India. That is because the crust is constantly being worn down (*eroded*) by wind, rain, ice, and other natural forces. Rocks exposed by this erosion gradually wear away into dust—except for hard materials such as diamonds. These remain as pebbles or chunks on the Earth's surface.

Many such diamonds are found

in the beds of rivers or streams. They are called *alluvial* diamonds (from an early Latin word meaning "to wash against").

Mining Diamonds

Most early diamond sources were alluvial, as in India and Brazil. Alluvial diamonds are still found today. Diamonds have been found in almost every state of the United States (especially Arkansas), for example, though they are usually small. Alluvial diamonds are also found in parts of Africa.

Individual miners sometimes scour streams and rivers to find diamond pebbles. For centuries some miners have built dams or canals to force water to take a different course. This exposes the streambed for easier mining.

Most diamonds today are found in mines dug below the surface, as in many diamond fields in southern Africa, Australia, and Russia. South Africa's Kimberley mine was dug so deep that it was nicknamed the Big Hole, before it was mined out and closed in 1914.

In major diamond fields, where diamond-bearing rock is found underground, miners using earthmoving equipment to dig up the whole area layer by layer, as at this open pit mine in Botswana, in south-central Africa.

This is a single day's production of rough diamonds from South Africa's Consolidated Diamond Mines. The whole mine operation of people and machines produced just 6,500 carats (a little less than three pounds) of diamonds on that one day, but these would be worth millions of dollars.

The largest modern mines use whole fleets of earthmoving equipment. These scour the earth, removing layer after layer of rock.

For shoreline fields, as on the coast of Namibia in southwest Africa, earthmovers sometimes create huge dikes to hold back the sea so miners can dig for diamonds. Mining ships also dig below the water to get at diamond-bearing rock offshore.

However and wherever it is found, the rock is put into crushing machines to be broken apart. The pieces then go through a series of washing and scouring processes.

The resulting pebbles and rock fragments are often put on a grease table—literally, a table coated with grease. The table is then flooded with water. Water washes away other stones, but diamonds stay in the grease. This works because diamond sheds water (like raindrops off a plastic raincoat) but attracts and is attracted to grease and oils. (That is why diamond pebbles found "in the rough" often feel greasy or waxy.)

Other Sources

Most diamonds being mined today were formed long ago, perhaps more than 3 billion years ago. We do not know if new diamonds are still being formed in the mantle.

Scientists have discovered that diamonds can be formed in the Earth in other ways. This can happen when an edge of the Earth's crust slides under another edge and is exposed to high pressure and temperature. The diamonds produced this way are very small ones called *microdiamonds*, sometimes measuring only about one-sixth the width of a human hair.

Some diamonds have also been formed in other parts of the universe. We know that because some meteorites (rocks from space) have been found to bear diamonds.

Humans have also learned how to make artificial diamonds (see below).

Many artificially made diamonds are used in industry, but some are also used in jewelry. Often no one but an expert can tell whether diamonds—like the one in this ring (left)—are real or artificial.

Artificial Diamonds

After many decades of trying, humans first made synthetic (artificial) diamonds in the 1950s. Scientists did this by putting graphite (see p. 6) under enormous pressure and temperatures as high as 1,700 degrees Celsius (3,100 Fahrenheit). Other researchers later developed different ways of producing artificial diamonds.

Today artificial diamonds make up about 80 percent of all diamonds used in industry. These are mostly small diamonds. The process is too expensive to make many very large diamonds.

Many artificial diamonds are also used in jewelry. However, the finest and most prized diamonds are still those made in nature.

A popular advertising slogan is "A diamond is forever." In modern times diamonds have become closely associated with engagements, weddings, and anniversaries. An engagement ring is often a single stone, called a *solitaire*, like the one shown here.

The Diamond Trade

Would you like to hold a fortune in your hand? Get a fistful of diamonds. They are so small, rare, beautiful, and valuable that a fistful would, indeed, be worth a fortune. Because of this, only highly trusted and carefully screened people are allowed to work with diamonds.

At the mines, specially trained workers clean, weigh, and count the rough diamonds. These are passed through sieves with holes of varying widths, so the diamonds are grouped by size.

The diamonds are then divided into two groups: gems and industrial diamonds. Diamonds that are too small or flawed for gem use are set aside for sale as industrial diamonds.

Within each size group gem-quality diamonds then go through

more careful sorting. Unbroken diamonds in regular shapes (see p. 7) are the most highly valued. Somewhat less prized are irregularly shaped diamonds, broken diamonds (*cleavages*), and triangle-shaped diamonds (*macles*; see p. 7). The least prized are flat, irregularly shaped diamonds, which look something like broken glass.

During sorting, the largest number of diamonds are usually cleavages. However, some of the largest and most famous diamonds were originally cleavages.

Next the gems are sorted for quality. Stones with flaws and

imperfections are less valuable. However, expert cutting can overcome some kinds of flaws (see p. 25).

Most diamonds are handled through the Diamond Producers Association, organized in the 1930s by the main South African diamond-mining companies. It sets production quotas (limits), controls prices, oversees the sorting and grading processes, and handles sales through its Central Selling Organization (CSO).

For sale by the CSO, the diamonds are sorted into packets called *sights*. Each contains dia-

Once separated and washed, diamonds are passed through sieves with holes of different sizes. Diamonds are passed first through the sieve with the widest holes (at left) and then those with smaller holes. As in most sorts, the largest number of diamonds are those of the smallest size (at right).

monds of a specified number, size, color, and shape. Packets can be worth a million dollars or more.

Such packets are sold at invitation-only sales (also called *sights*) held ten times a year. Only specially approved buyers (*sight holders*)—generally fewer than 200 in the world—can attend such sales.

The sight holders then sell diamonds to other buyers at diamond markets in cities around the world, most notably Antwerp, Belgium; Bombay, India; London, England; Amsterdam, the Netherlands; New York City; Tel Aviv, Israel; Bangkok, Thailand; and Singapore. Only then are diamonds sold to people who will cut them for sale to customers (see p. 25).

Australian diamonds, formerly sold this way, have from the 1990s been sold primarily through India. That country is once again a leader in the diamond trade, especially in cutting diamonds and in making diamond jewelry.

The finest diamonds are clear and colorless, like this one. They are sometimes said to be "of the first water" because they look like the clearest springwater.

The Four C's

The value of a diamond gemstone depends on the four C's:

Clarity: The stone should be clear and without flaws.

Color: The most prized are clear and colorless, but colored stones (fancies) are also valued.

Cut: Diamonds are cut to increase light and color.

Carat weight: Large diamonds are the most valued.

Shaping Diamonds

Before cleaving a diamond, diamond experts study its internal structure using magnifiers, so they know precisely where to strike. This view of the internal structure of a diamond has been enlarged 75 times.

In early times diamonds were only polished. This removed a "skin" of dirt and other substances. Because they are so hard, diamonds can only be polished by other diamonds.

The polishing process, called *bruting*, was done by hand until the 1660s, when a diamond-coated polishing wheel was developed. The wheel was called a *lap*, so jewelers came to be called *lapidaries*.

From about 1330, possibly starting in Venice, Italy, some jewelers began to experiment with cutting diamonds. Cutting techniques then traveled throughout Europe and Asia.

Cutting Diamonds

Diamonds must be cut with great knowledge and care. Although extremely hard, diamonds are also brittle. They can be destroyed if they are hit in the wrong way.

Jewelers analyze the internal structure of diamonds under a magnifying glass (*loupe*) before deciding precisely where to cut a stone (see photo above). If a gem has a flaw,

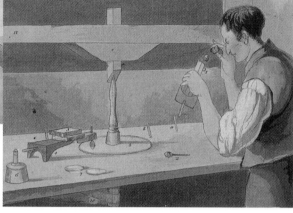

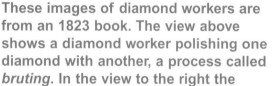

These images of diamond workers are from an 1823 book. The view above shows a diamond worker polishing one diamond with another, a process called *bruting*. In the view to the right the worker is preparing to cut a diamond, while another diamond is being polished on the wheel (*lap*) to his left. Though new technology, such as motors and lasers, is now used in working with diamonds, the essential procedures remain the same.

the jeweler can sometimes cut it to remove the flaw.

The jeweler marks the diamond using a pen, another diamond, or today a laser (high-intensity light beam). Using another diamond, the jeweler makes a cut along the mark and places a steel wedge into the cut. If all goes well, the jeweler then *cleaves* (splits) the diamond by hitting the wedge with a mallet (light hammer), the way a woodcutter splits a piece of wood.

Large stones may be cut into several gems. One of the largest chunks of diamond ever found was the Cullinan diamond (named for the mine owner), discovered in

South Africa in 1905. An amazing 3,106 carats (about 1.3 pounds) and measuring 4 by 2.5 by 2.5 inches, it was almost as big as a man's fist.

Dutch diamond expert Joseph Asscher studied the Cullinan for several months. The first time he tried to cut it, the steel blade broke, and the diamond remained whole. The second time the diamond split into three sections as he had planned—though the strain was so great that Asscher fainted!

The final result was several large stones and a number of smaller ones, all now part of England's Crown Jewels. Among these were the Cullinan I (at 530.2 carats) and

Cullinan II, the largest known cut stones before the Golden Jubilee (see p. 10).

A diamond-edged circular saw may be used to further shape a diamond or to cut one unsuitable for cleaving. After creating the basic shape they want, jewelers use bruting to create a more precise shape, including many small, flat, highly polished surfaces (*facets*). The aim is to produce the maximum amount of light and color in the final cut diamonds (see p. 9).

Over the centuries jewelers have developed many kinds of shapes and patterns of facets, called *cuts*. The *brilliant cut*, developed in the mid-1700s and improved since then, remains the most popular.

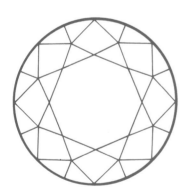
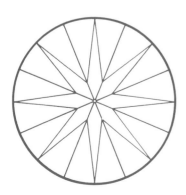

These drawings (left) show the standard modern cut of a round brilliant diamond, like the one shown here below. The drawings show the views from the side, the top, and the bottom.

This sparkling diamond is an example of the popular *brilliant cut*. In early times the pointed bottom of the diamond was enclosed in metal. Today jewelers use several prongs to hold gemstones in rings, leaving the rest of the bottom open to receive more light, increasing the sparkle.

The two small diamonds in this diamond anvil—shown much magnified—serve as a clamp or vise. The material being studied is put into the sealed compartment (the dark area) between them and then squeezed, so scientists can study how it changes under high pressure.

The Many Uses of Diamonds

As the hardest material known, diamond has many uses. Diamonds seem to have been used for drilling beads by at least 400 B.C. They were also used from early times to engrave designs and words onto other precious stones, including diamonds.

Diamonds continued to be widely used for cutting and grinding, and that is still true today. When you see someone operating a cutting wheel to carve up a cement sidewalk, chances are the wheel is edged with diamonds. When you see a prospector drilling for oil or a machine punching deep into the earth for a sample of ice or rock, it is likely that the tip of the drill bit is covered with diamonds.

Similarly, when you see a machine used to grind down or polish other hard materials, the grinding or polishing wheel may very well be covered with diamond sand. (Such a wheel would not be used

Diamond-studded drill bits like the ones shown here are widely used in drilling for oil and natural gas. The many hard diamonds help to cut through rock to reach valuable underground deposits.

squeeze the diamonds together to study how it changes under very high pressure.

Because they are both hard and clear, diamonds were used as early as 1978 to make the windows in a spacecraft sent to explore other parts of our solar system. Diamonds have also been made into thin, clear, hard films for special uses.

for soft materials, though, because the diamonds would probably tear them apart.)

Today diamonds have many other uses, some of them in high-technology fields. One of the most extraordinary uses of diamonds is in tiny anvils (clamps or vises with two "jaws"). A pair of diamonds with flat tops (*tables*) are placed together with a tiny sealed space between them (see image on p. 28). Scientists put the substance being studied in that tiny space and

Artificial diamonds are widely used in industry. These are diamond dies (shaping devices). Metal is forced through a hole in the center of the diamond, making telephone wire of even width.

Words to Know

alluvial diamonds Diamonds found near streams or other waterways, exposed by the work of EROSION.

anvil In diamonds a type of small clamp or vise with two "jaws" formed by diamonds. Substances are placed in the anvil and put under high pressure so that scientists can study them.

artificial (synthetic) diamonds Diamonds made by humans. Most industrial diamonds today are artificial, as are some diamonds used in jewelry.

atom A basic "building block" of nature. In an ELEMENT, such as CARBON, all the atoms are alike.

bruting Polishing or grinding a precious stone. Diamonds can only be bruted by another diamond.

carat A basic measure of weight used for diamonds and other precious stones. A carat is equivalent to .2 grams (200 milligrams). Smaller weights are measured in POINTS. (In precious metals a karat or carat is a measure of purity.)

carbon (C) One of the universe's basic ELEMENTS. Diamonds are made of pure carbon.

Central Selling Organization (CSO) An arm of the Diamond Producers Association founded in the 1930s to control the production and sale of diamonds. The stones are offered for sale at SIGHTS.

cleavages Broken diamonds. Diamonds that are split deliberately by jewelers are said to be *cleaved*. This is done to prepare a diamond for further shaping and cutting.

crystal A solid material that is made up of regular three-dimensional units repeated over and over. Both diamond and GRAPHITE are crystals.

cut A design for creating many small, flat, highly polished surfaces (FACETS) on a diamond to increase its light and brilliance. Among the many modern cuts the most popular is the *brilliant cut*.

elements The basic materials that make up every living and nonliving thing in the universe. In an element all the ATOMS are alike.

erosion The wearing away of the Earth's crust by wind, rain, ice, and other natural forces. This process can expose diamonds.

facets Small, flat, highly polished surfaces made in diamonds, designed to increase their brilliant light and color.

fancy A colored diamond.

Four C's A guide to the value of a diamond: Clarity, Color, Cut, and Carat weight.

graphite A material of pure CARBON, like diamond, but with a different structure and so not as hard.

kimberlite pipes Long, thin formations of diamond-bearing rocks, named for South Africa's Kimberley mine.

lap The BRUTING wheel used to grind and polish diamonds. The people who used such a wheel were traditionally called *lapidaries*.

loupe A small magnifying glass used by jewelers and others.

macles Diamonds shaped roughly like thick triangles (three-sided figures).

mantle The layer below the crust of the Earth. Most diamonds were formed there under great heat and pressure.

octahedron An eight-sided figure, like two PYRAMIDS placed bottom to bottom. It is the classic and most valued shape of a diamond CRYSTAL.

pipes: See KIMBERLITE PIPES.

point A small measure of weight in diamonds. One point equals .01 CARATS.

pyramid A solid figure with four upper faces shaped like triangles (three-sided figures) and a square face (a shape with four equal sides) on the bottom. The classic diamond shape, the OCTAHEDRON, is like two pyramids placed bottom to bottom.

sand In the jeweler's world tiny fragments of diamond used for grinding and polishing diamonds and other substances.

sight A packet of diamonds put together for sale by the CENTRAL SELLING ORGANIZATION; also the invitation-only sale where such packets are sold. The limited number of buyers at these sales are called *sight holders*.

synthetic diamonds: See ARTIFICIAL DIAMONDS.

On the Internet

The Internet has many interesting sites about diamonds. The site addresses often change, so the best way to find current addresses is to go to a search site, such as www.yahoo.com. Type in a word or phrase, such as "diamond."

As this book was being written, websites about diamonds included:

http://www.amnh.org/exhibitions/diamonds/
The Nature of Diamonds, an online exhibit from the American Museum of Natural History.

http://www.si.edu/resource/faq/nmnh/hope.htm
The Hope Diamond, a page from the Smithsonian Institution.

http://magma.nationalgeographic.com/ngm/data/2002/03/01/sights_n_sounds/media.1.2.html
Diamonds: The Real Story, from the National Geographic Society.

http://www.pbs.org/wgbh/nova/diamond/
The Diamond Deception, from Nova Online.

http://csd.unl.edu/csd/birthstones/diamonds/diamond.html
Diamond as the April birthstone, from the University of Nebraska–Lincoln.

http://www.AllAboutJewels.com/jewel/
All About Jewels: Illustrated Dictionary of Jewelry, part of EnchantedLearning.com.

In Print

Your local library system will have various books on diamonds. The following is just a sampling of them.

Bruton, Eric. *Diamonds*, 2d ed. Radnor, PA: Chilton, 1978.
Diamonds: Myth, Magic, and Reality. Ronne Peltzman and Neil Grant, eds. New York: Crown, 1980.
Dickinson, Joan. *The Book of Diamonds*. New York: Crown, 1965.
Green, Timothy. *The World of Diamonds*. New York: Morrow, 1981.
Hart, Matthew. *Diamond: A Journey to the Heart of an Obsession*. New York: Walker, 2001.
Koskoff, David E. *The Diamond World*. New York: Harper & Row, 1981.
Legrand, Jacques. *Diamonds: Myth, Magic and Reality*. New York: Crown, 1980.
Nature of Diamonds, The. George E. Harlow, ed. New York: Cambridge University Press in association with the American Museum of Natural History, 1998.
Stwertka, Albert. *Oxford Guide to the Elements*. New York: Oxford, 1998.
Tillander, Herbert. *Diamond Cuts in Historic Jewellery 1381–1910*. London: Arts Books International, 1995.
Van Nostrand's Scientific Encyclopedia, 8th ed., 2 vols. Douglas M. Considine and Glenn D. Considine, eds. New York: Van Nostrand Reinhold, 1995.

Index